Stripes & Polka Dots

STANIELLA OTHELLO

authorHOUSE®

AuthorHouse™
1663 Liberty Drive
Bloomington, IN 47403
www.authorhouse.com
Phone: 1 (800) 839-8640

Published by AuthorHouse   05/25/2017

ISBN: 978-1-5246-9388-6 (sc)
ISBN: 978-1-5246-9387-9 (e)

Library of Congress Control Number: 2017908379

Print information available on the last page.

Any people depicted in stock imagery provided by Thinkstock are models, and such images are being used for illustrative purposes only. Certain stock imagery © Thinkstock.

This book is printed on acid-free paper.

Because of the dynamic nature of the Internet, any web addresses or links contained in this book may have changed since publication and may no longer be valid. The views expressed in this work are solely those of the author and do not necessarily reflect the views of the publisher, and the publisher hereby disclaims any responsibility for them.

Preamble

I am learning to live unapologetically.
I can boldly speak my truths.
I don't have to fear my darker parts.
I own my weaknesses.
I own my strengths.
I don't have to make myself small.
I don't have to make myself big.
I don't have to make myself fit
or occupy spaces I don't want to.
I can just be: however & whatever that means.

--Staniella

Contents

Crenglish.. 1

Westview.. 3

Seat Fillers... 4

Escape Routes 5

What Reeves Taught Me.. 6

Appropriation... 7

Lost Girls 8

Anxious Creature 10

Fear & Carnage 11

Ayiti Cherie... 12

Never Been Loved... 14

Hands 15

Midnight.. 16

False Alarms... 18

Mama's Superstitions...19

Warm & Deep 20

Affection 21

Inherent Patterns.. 22

Band-Aids 23

Manman'm Te Di / My Mother Said 25

Fear of Abandonment... 27

Pep Mwen 28

Stereotypical 30

Transracial 32

Chasing Dragons 34

Heartbreak Kid 36

Insecure 38

Rider 39

Collide With Me 40

Dashes, Hyphens, & Minuses 41

Rhythm 43

Calls 44

Grieve 46

Love Him Like… 48

Joy 50

Ode to Andre 51

Words 53

If Walls Could Talk 55

Energy (A Poem for Morales) 56

Call Center Resources 58

Thank you 60

Unfair Trades 62

Crenglish

We gesticulate when we tell stories.
Smiles wide, we speak using our whole bodies
We laugh loudly and yes,
sometimes it sounds like we're arguing but we're not.
We wear polka dots and stripes
and you cannot tell us that we're not fre.
I mean fresh.
Nou toujou bien abiye,
Well-dressed rocking Zoe man sandals.
Nou pap kite entranje yo di nou ke nou pap sove
paske survival is in our DNA.
Those strangers know nothing about us,
how dare they say we can't be saved?
Nou se moun fò;
we are a strong people.
We are bold.
We are hustlers.
We are proud.
We may not have mastered the English language
but we've mastered heart.
We will put tout bagay on de line
pou yon chans for de better lye-eef—Life.
We take chances at it.
We put everything on the line
to make something out of the nothing we came with.
Béniswa Leténél.
Blessed is the Lord,
our tongues know the language
of praise and worship.
We are the melting pot;
the spirit of Independence.
The heart of Freedom;

We are the rebellion,
Haters can never stop us,
lènmi nou pa ka sispann nou.
Nap etidye tout sa nou bezwen
pou nou ka akonpli rèv Ameriken sa.
We will study everything we need
to accomplish the American dream.
Grace a dieu.
Nou pa bezwen pale angle tankou ekspè,
we don't have to be experts at English,
we jes need to talkin' angle klè enuf.
Clear enough for them to see us trying.
Accents heavy but our diligence weighs more.
There's cunning in our bones
and persistence on our tongues.
There is a tenacity coursing through our veins.
We want to make good;
We want better for our children.
We give up degrees and prestigious occupations;
humble ourselves to housekeepers and cashiers,
janitors and gravediggers
for a better life here—for a chance.
We trade our certifications for opportunities for our children
so they can have better lives.
We blend our Creole with your English.
We speak Crenglish.

Westview

My friends drink Smirnoff,
skip school,
sell weed,
steal cars,
have sex for money.
My friends skateboard,
ride bicycles,
sell DVDs,
love the theater,
love to dance,
write poetry.
We get into the clubs free.
We go to day parties and get lifted.
We think we're deep.
We dance and break curfew.
It's lame to be a virgin.
It's a shame not to have a sugar daddy.
Skillset: tease.
We get our nails done,
we cop outfits,
we ride shotgun.
Skillset: hold hair and purses,
keep everyone out of trouble.
Avoid catching stray bullets.
Pine after our favorite poets
and protest injustice.
Manage grades;
obsess over passing standardized tests
and living up to superlatives.
All while finding a way to be free.

Seat Fillers

To see you is not to know you.
I don't know you,
so seeing you makes my heart ache.
Stomach turns into a sea of knots when those kids
who share the same half of you as me
say your name because I can't relate to this
"Daddy" that they speak of.
Stories of how over-bearing you can be
made the hole in me burn with envy
because I never had the chance
to have you to get on my nerves.
No father to sit with and read stories,
so I settled for sugar daddies instead.
Breaking everything good in me
hoping that maybe I'd find a glimpse of
what you were supposed to be for me.
Instead, I was broken in vain.
Self-destructed 'til I realized that the
You I needed would never be manifested.
Collected my broken, corroded pieces
and placed them in the empty hole reserved for you
along with the labels of the missing pieces
I let worthless men take from me.
Maybe if I knew you,
it could've all been different.
But, in chasing my idea of
who you were supposed to be,
I cried myself to sleep counting off my list
of shouldn't haves instead of all those
maybes.

Escape Routes

I joined the navy because my recruiter told me
that I could be an actor there,
said I could be a poet, a writer there,
there were programs to help me hone my craft.
He said to check out MWR when I got to my duty station,
they could make anything happen.
No lie, he said those things with a straight face.
Told me I'd get paid for speaking another language,
convinced me to enlist as an engineer,
because my ASVAB scores indicated
that I was mechanically inclined
and they needed more black women in the field.
He told me I'd be a trailblazer.
(He was a liar, obviously.)
I joined the navy because Somali was going.
He said he was gonna be a chef or something.
He wasn't scared to serve his country
and make this money.
He didn't know it but he was a god to me.
I had no dreams other than getting out of Miami,
making a name for myself and being in his dreams.
His dreads were long, my eyes were big
and my hollow heart naïve.
Broken I was searching for validation everywhere
and if he said the Navy could accelerate his life,
then it could help mine too, dammit.
He cut his hair and I thought,
Oh snap! They making him a man already,
Let me gon' ahead and be great too.
I joined the Navy 'cause I thought
I would be safe there.
(I lied to myself, too.)

What Reeves Taught Me

You are not allowed to change your mind.
You cannot say no if you've already said yes.
You can't decide that you don't want to do this anymore in the middle of
already doing it.
You cannot say stop after saying go
It don't work like that shawty.
You can't just change your mind during sex.

(Get off me.
Please, I don't want this.
I want to go home.)

Shut up, you gon take this!
Why you running?
Ain't this what you wanted?

(NO!)

You been frontin like I couldn't hit.
Wait till I tell my boys about this.

(Stop it. Just let me go.)

No, you don't get to change your mind.
This is mine & and Imma take it.

Enter outer body experience.
Floating outside of myself watching, as something heavy within
shattered.
Tears spilling as my throat grew tight and hoarse.
Looking down on myself like
What did you get yourself into?
Why did you think for a second that coming in here was a good idea?
Where did everyone else go?
Why won't he just hurry up and finish so you can go.
Stop crying.
Turn every emotion off it'll hurt less that way.
You can clean up when we get home.

Appropriation

They keep jockin' our styles.
Appropriating our culture and calling it theirs,
copyright infringement on our lifestyles
while they listen to lifestyle
talking about "it's my life, man".
They'd pay to play black,
get paid to play black,
don't understand that
blackface is not innocent,
It's not jest or emulation;
Melanin is not a punchline.
They want us to fall in line.
They want our lines.
They want our lives.
Want to play our roles-
share the experience without the struggle -
they call copying our hustle thinking outside the box.
The box they put us in the first place.
Compare us to crabs in buckets
conveniently forgetting that buckets
aren't a crab's natural habitat.
They're so scared of a revolution
I guess that's why they try so hard
why they shoot, rob and kill us.
I'm telling you they're trigger happy
because they're scared of
what we could do if we decide to get buck.
If they were us, they'd tear this whole place up.
(The proof is in the MayFlower and Plymouth Rock.)

Lost Girls

This is for the lost girls.
Insecure girls.
The ones who seek validation
through likes on the internet,
those who so badly yearn for affection
they search for it in sexting.
For the rebels and the runaways,
those who've been assaulted,
corrupted and refuse to see themselves as victims.
Gritty
Detached
Cold
Those girls who are always on the run,
rushing to become women
because their childhoods failed them,
this is for you.
Butterfly with clipped wings;
bumble bee without stinger
the one's made to feel broken; insufficient.
Ugly
Dirty
The one's who hustle,
using bodies and drugs as currency—
using struggle to keep their heads held high.
For the misguided in 6 inch heels,
for bag ladies,
for the ones who don't know what love is
but look for it in bumming smokes
and someone else's kisses,
the ones who've witnessed
the closed fist to chest kind of love.
The ones who've been 16 and pregnant

without the glitz or glamour of MTV.
The ones traded by their mamas,
drifting on clouds to forget.
For the cutters trying to relieve themselves
of the pressure and the pain,
the thigh gap obsessed,
the anorexic and bulimic,
the ones who can't see through
the rainbow glare of their tears.
The ones drowning themselves in booze,
over-eaters seeking refuge in food
this is for you.
You don't have to be lost anymore.
Your imperfections make you perfectly who you are,
you can stop running.
You're not alone.
Come home,
you don't have to hurt anymore.

Anxious Creature

I am so afraid of arguments
So panicky about conflict
that I bite my tongue and tuck in my ~~tail~~ spine.
I do not like to rock the boat.
I ~~run away from~~ avoid chaos.
Hyper vigilant,
I'm anxious ridden in crowds
especially crowds of emotions.
Though I may grumble and ~~growl~~ complain often,
I'm careful of my audience,
terrified of the power in my ~~bite~~ reactions.
I do not like to be noticed.
I've been abused and misconstrued ~~like dogs~~.
I've been goaded.
Baited.
~~Trained~~ Primed to respond and defend,
that I play offense so often,
so much, I can't really trust my own ~~scent~~ judgment.
Everyone is a threat.
No one is a friend.
I don't want to ~~be feral~~ live like that.
I don't want to be so anxious and wild that I keep
fighting to censor and tame myself.
I want to be free.

Fear & Carnage

Conditioned to go for the jugular,
I was bred for demolition.
Tempered to wreak havoc.
Tongue sharp and cutthroat,
primed to cause carnage
Hands to the ready,
trigger finger poised for the pull.
Legs strong for the jump.
Heart distant and unyielding.
There was no post to the trauma.
Can't remember what the pre felt like,
I've been in the thick of it
a very long time
even if it's just in my mind
so I learned to keep it all in.
Smothered it.
Battened down the hatches
to keep the rage from escaping.
Learned to channel it into laughter,
jokes, poems, sarcasm so heavy
I think I became scorn.
Have you ever seen an animal forget its majesty?
Go feral?
Forget that there was once peace?
Have you any idea what it's like to feel
as though you're always at war?
I am afraid.
Petrified of the savagery in my blood.
The ire in my veins,
umbrage under my skin.
The capacity to break backbone
and reinforce it with zero f**ks,
and turn my humanity off.
Unperturbed by the cost.

11

Ayiti Cherie

We saw them struggling.
Trying to find an expressway to escape
to lands of opportunity.
Never mind political asylum,
they needed refuge from being refugees,
came in search of Peace
or maybe just a piece of the dream
but it seems for many the dream has been deferred.
In search of a home that they would never find;
bereft in their quest for peace of mind.
Trapped beneath slabs of concrete.
Bodies bent by collapsed buildings,
but it could never break their spirits or
willingness to survive.
In a world so consumed in darkness,
they still held up a light,
heads to the heavens and the hills
from which their help comes.
Vessels broken but their hearts
will never come undone.
Despite their distress,
their prayers will never go unsung,
they strive to be better than their situation.
Broadcasters reporting that Haiti needs aide,
but turned a blind eye before the earth quaked,
though they knew the suffrage existed
long before then.
Self-proclaimed "self-made" men
degraded a nation because of its circumstance.
They said we had this coming.
False prophets claimed we sold our soul to the devil
so we deserved to be in ruins.

In a time of distress,
as we tried to pick up the pieces left
we still had antagonists making up our sins,
proving the "united we stand, divided we fall" mentality
falls short towards the rest of humanity.
One nation under but the same christians
live apart from their religion.
Body of Christ with a little "c".
No wonder we can't see the God in them.
Blinded by egos they believe they're gods
among men, unwilling to assist those who
won't worship at their altar.
They didn't need an earthquake to know
they could have some something more.
Though she may physically be in ruins understand her spirit is not broken.
Ayiti has already survived so much;
She knows there is no giving up.
It's going to take a lot more to leave her rattled.

Never Been Loved

I've never been loved before, not for real.
I've had promises that resulted in empty,
I've had taken for granted, used, made to feel cheap,
but I've never had I love you.
Sure, I've heard the words spoken
but never really lived out.
I've had hindsight, last ditch efforts,
attempts but I've never had love.
I've been property.
Possession, territory, convenience, afterthought,
mistake, ruse, game.
Everything in between and everything short of
but I've never been loved.
I've had proposals, a baby,
promises so broken that when put back together,
even they don't remember themselves.
I've had the kind of I love you's
used car salesman sells—Lemons.
I've made more than my share of lemonade,
I'm over the acidity, the tartness of a fickle heart.
Just give me water; give me pure.
Basic and necessary, no frills or disguises.
I've heard lies that tasted like truth,
I'm so over the Splenda and Equal,
artificial sweeteners, I want it raw.
I've wanted the real thing for as long as I could remember,
I sometimes wonder if even that's real.
I'm beginning to believe charming and sincere cannot coexist,
I just want to be loved.
In action like verb; with purpose.
I just want to be loved.

Hands

I used to be joked for my height
and the size of my hands.
Made to feel ashamed…disproportionate.
Inferior for things I couldn't change
like my complexion.
Seldom was I just pretty-
mostly pretty for a dark-skinned girl.
It took a while to love myself: buckteeth and curls
even though the former I've set straight.
I used to feel awkward.
Sometimes I still do,
when I realize that the size of my hands
rival those of some dudes
but what matters is what these hands do.
They straighten crowns.
They have wiped bottoms & noses; blood & sweat,
they've wiped away tears.
They've rubbed backs & held bodies,
held hands & rubbed feet,
held on to & burped babies.
These hands hold hearts & handles them with care,
tilt chins up when crowns get heavy,
they smooth out hair, shape dreams & rub bellies,
scare away monsters sock puppet silly,
these hands cook & bake,
clean &write,
gesture & dap,
tickle & shake
comfort & caress
even if sometimes they sweat with the labor
these gargantuan hands offer reprieve.
These hands love, fight, bleed and
I wouldn't make them smaller for anything.
(About these feet though?)

Midnight

It's midnight & I get a phone call.
My cousin's screaming her dude's gonna knock her top off and she's scared.
I jump out of the bed,
hop into my work boots & sweats,
jump into the Intrepid,
speakers blastin' behind mirror tint
thinking this is insane.
Jazmine Sullivan's "Call Me Guilty" song is playing,
Smith & Wesson in my lap.
How hard is it for this clown to learn his lesson?
He's already been pistol whipped.
Maybe the lesson didn't take.
Pushing 100 on the highway
I've got to make it to his street,
to the blue house on the corner of 135th & 10th;
I pop the trunk open, grab the tire iron & crowbar
lay them on the side of the car in case I need them.
Grab my mace and Mr. Smith
If there's even a faint trace of blue
or a scratch on her face, he's dead.
I'm here for his head,
I'm tired of seeing her black & blue.
I approach the door & her yelling continues
He's chasing her across the room,
butcher knife in hand,
demanding that she bow down.
A shot's fired.
Behind the sound of shattered glass
I can hear the coward screaming.
I kick the door in,
I hear exclamations and heavy breathing.
I scan the room & my vision lands on my cousin,

her beautiful brown eyes are swollen shut.
Her face is a deep purple & her lip is busted up,
her clothes are torn, hair disheveled &
she scampers to the other side of the room whispering,
"he tried to rape me...again".
I'm trying not to let my fury run rampant
but the muzzle of my gun is already in his mouth.
A sick laugh escapes me.
I know I'd pull the trigger if he tries me.
His eye twitches.
In a quick motion
He lunges and I squeeze.
My cousin screams,
stumbling towards the stairs.
I run past her,
rushing to get the kids.
I find them scared, huddled in a corner.
We coax them out to safety.
It's 11:23 pm.
Something stirs me from sleep.
I'm covered in sweat
and I can hear my heartbeat thumping in my ears.
I feel a chill in the room and dread lingers.
I lie awake watching the clock thinking,
I'd better not have to live that nightmare tonight.

False Alarms

I run into burning buildings.
Heart first
love enough for all of us
even though my lungs can't always handle the smoke.
Eyes water and blur at the thought of someone else's hurt…
I run into burning buildings.
Despite my training and know how
I still try to put out electrical fires with the hose,
suffering third degree burns in the name of always being there.
I leap to rescue.
(I lose sleep)
Heart on my sleeve.
(I bend spine)
Mind frantic.
(Run red lights)
All in the name of being loyal
only to discover there was no emergency.
It was just a little smoke.
battered
broken
bruised
burned
behind what I imagine friendship to be.
The impulse to always be sanctuary weighs heavily on my soul.
I race to rescue and put myself in jeopardy.
When will I learn that before I save anyone else,
I've got to save myself?
When will I learn?

Mama's Superstitions

• • • • • • • • ● ○ ○ ○ ○ ○ ○ ○ ○ ○ ○

"3 am is the hour of the devil..."

Mummy, how do you know this?

"Depression is a weakness..."

No mom, it's a mental illness.

"At night if you hear someone call your name, don't answer. It's the devil..."

Or it could be a person I know...

"There are crazy people hiding in bushes
waiting to rape and kill you."

Thanks for the unhealthy fear of bushes.

"What happens if you go to that party and end up in a ditch somewhere?"

Why do your scenarios have me in ditches?

"Put these batteries in your pockets..."

I did it. I still don't know why, but I did it.

"Walking around with one shoe on
will cause your mother to die."

I'm pretty sure
that's not how death works.

"If a cleaning broom sweeps your feet you will never marry."

I've wiped my feet on *so* many brooms.
(I's married now though. Sooooo.)

Warm & Deep

I have a confession.
I love you.
So much that I feel it in my bones,
deep in my marrow.
I love you like an infection.
I love you like gangrene.
Goodness, I just love you so much!
I used to love you like I loved lilies.
That was before I received a repurposed bouquet
of crushed lilies two days after valentine's and found panties that weren't
mine in your bed.
I used to love you.
Like I used to love Shakespeare's Romeo;
how I thought he spoke the sweetest words.
Now, I love you like children love disappointments
and another set of hand-me-downs.
It turns out all your "love" was handed down
to me when she didn't want it
and I'd rather have a love unrequited than accept
a half-assed, misappropriated kind of love.
You can keep this "thing" we had
that bring you to me and your second-hand antonym
rebirthed into the word for "a feeling of warm, personal attachment or
deep affection".
I have a feeling of
"warmth and deep affection" for you too.
It's most potent in my two middle fingers.

Affection

●●●●●●●●●○○○○○○○○ ○ ○

She doesn't love you.
Like daggers her hateful words slip over her tongue,
stabbing past the walls of her teeth and the shield of
her lips to pierce deep into your spirit.
She tears you down with the cannons of her rejection and their turrets.
She degrades you...
She slanders love and commits crimes of defamation against its
character when she uses it in vain.
She uses "I love you" like a curse.
You take her poison in all the forms she gives it in
Only to stumble into the hospital of my chest,
expecting my loyalty & affection to render you whole.
You bring your "I Love You".
Her "screw you" dusted off,
shaped into butterflies and rainbows by your lips.
Four-leaf clovers & unicorns, your tongue
sleeks past ivory walls of teeth to spew it,
refurbished with whispers and kisses that leave an ironic taste in my
mouth.
You take her manure and use it to give me roses
failing to realize that roses smell like betrayal.
You take the blood from your wounds and brush it over fresh white
petals expecting me
to take them as a symbol of your affection.
Expect me to accept them.
You expect me to "play my position"
for the home team.
Trouble is,
I'm a free agent.
I play for me.

Inherent Patterns

I'm my mother's daughter.
That's how it seems,
for surely I've made the same mistakes.
Mistakes like counting on love to carry me through.
Mistakes like believing that I could find the Me in you.
Mistakes so circular they practically make my existence redundant.
Re-runs of "I've got daddy Issues",
Episodes of "I'm emotionally damaged"
looking to fix the broken
so I'm not the one being fixed.
Daddy like traits cause me to call it quits when I'm faced with love.
Running at the first sign of commitment
even though love is all
I
ever
think
of.
Seat-fillers in this ache in me.
Posers I allowed to stick around 'til one of us got tired
and no matter how many times I said I wouldn't let history repeat itself,
here we are.
Here
I
am.
My Mother's child;
my father's daughter.

Band-Aids

We use "I love you" like Band-Aids.
Apply "I'm sorry" like a salve,
we don't know how to let ourselves
heal like we ought to.
We dress our scars; pick at scabs.
We never really grasped how to let our wounds be
so even when they begin to heal
we reopen them for attention.
Our battle scars beg people to listen to their stories
but we never really have much to tell,
we're just proud we survived at all.
We want to feel alive so we reach out to and cling on to someone else,
someone that'll share in our dysfunction.
Smother our burns with butter
with the pretense of healing
but instead end up paving a road
with good intentions.
We put egg whites on burns to relieve our pain,
get over the last by getting under someone else,
further injuring ourselves because
we don't want to feel.
We get over breakups
by diving head first into relationships
and call them love instead of rebounds.
Stab at the sore on our souls
to feel something real again.
Lose ourselves in drink, smoke, pills
and sex to numb the ache.
We don't cool off.
We're too cool even
when it's obvious we're stressed;
we put ice on our emotions and swan dive into something new;

something different.
We mask our pain in cynicism
fill our voids with temporary fixes,
anything to dull the pain within our chests.
We're so addicted to the thrill of "I love you
and the security it promises
that we chase the dragon
of what could've been with someone else.
Make wishes on fallen eyelashes.
Look for shooting stars,
stare down the clock waiting for 11:11.
Bury our hearts in maladaptive coping skills
searching for an epic love.
We look for the Band-Aid that'll never come off.
Most of all, that the next person will be the one to keep their promises.

Manman'm Te Di / My Mother Said

Ou bel.
Ou gen lespri.
Ou se lògèy ak kè kontan nan fanmi sa a.
ou se fason n'ap soti nan mizè sa a.
Mwen kache tout rèv mwen yo nan ou
Seyè a konnen ou se sove nou
men se li ki delivre nou.
Ou se manifestasyon rèv mwen ak tout espwa m.
Ou se potansyèl kri
ou gen chans pou reyisi rive nan tout bagay mwen pa t kapab
ou'ap vin yon fanm.
Yon fanm tankou fanm mwen te ye a
feròs
superbe efikas
ekonomik
entelijan
anfom toutbon
W ap jwenn yon mari
sa kap ofri ou rich ak sekirite.
Ou'ap ka ofri tout bagay sa yo ban mwen.
Lè sa a, nou pral reyalize tout bagay.

You are beautiful.
You have smarts.
You are the pride and joy of this family.
you are our way out of poverty.
I have hidden all of my dreams in you.
Lord knows you are our rescue
and He is our salvation.
You are the manifestation of my dreams and all of my hopes.
You are unabridged potential
You have the opportunity to achieve everything I couldn't

You will become a woman
the woman I used to be
fierce
gorgeous
efficient
economical
intelligent
sexy
You will find a husband.
He will provide you wealth, security,
and you will be able to offer those things to me
and then, we will accomplish everything.

Fear of Abandonment

I'm afraid.
Afraid to embrace proposals of forever because maybe
he'll wake up beside me one day and realize that
forever is just too much and leave.
Like
you
did.
Pretend I never existed
and move on with someone borrowed,
steal their forever and return mine to sender.
I wish you could explain it.
Maybe if I could wrap my head around your
abandonment and fickle nature
I could break this destructive cycle in me.
Maybe I could find peace and stop running in circles.
Trust someone with my heart.
Trust someone with love.
Give a man with the power to love me
the benefit of the doubt
but instead I'm stuck here trying to figure me out
with no clues and empty boxes of you.
Single parent pictures of my mother and I
have become single parent pictures
of me and my son.
A son who gives me cards on Father's Day,
begs to spend weekends with Grandpa,
a man who is still a father I never knew.
You.
And I'm just supposed to let him love you
when I have no idea who it is you really are.

Pep Mwen

My people.
My people have been seeking refuge for so long
they have been so strong in the face of adversity.
They know how to make the world their own
how to make beauty from ashes
how to worship in the midst of the trial.
They were forged by fire.
Courage runs deep in their blood
independence hard fought and hard won
don't let the media convince you
it was just about soup.
When was the last time you saw an uprising
leave a people feeling so beautiful?
They don't hide their scars.
They have no need for scapegoats.
They shoulder their burdens
and never let the weight crush their spirit
these are my people.
Their blood lives in my veins, they dance, laugh, sing
and nurture the soil of their land.
They know the merit of hard labor.
The spoils of love.
They walk with their heads high,
spine straight, shoulders broad,
they carry wisdom in their hearts
and survival on their heads,
they are not afraid to work and play.
Wash their burdens and sins in the river they are
not afraid to live and pray,
don't let these missionaries try to convince you
that my people are tainted by voodoo.
They are inherently black magic because: melanin.

They ain't ever needed saving or rescue,
maybe a little refuge but let me tell you
Pep mwen!
My people have always been good at
saving themselves.
They don't crack under pressure.
They expand.
Don't let that earthquake fool you.
Don't let the tyrants confuse you,
we ain't ever been scared of machetes or politics.
We carry freedom and cutthroat in our veins.
We carry rebellion and revolution in our DNA
We carry love and hope as natural
and sweet as sugar cane.
We ain't afraid to get back up again.
We are more than the summation
of first world views and televangelists.
We have survived the reckoning.
L'Union Fait La Force
Unity Makes Strength.

Stereotypical

They would have you believe that we're all out here smacking and rolling our necks.
Twerking, not working, using section 8 for rent,
regaling you with enough truTV to buy the hype.
Fake like how full lips are officially cool now that Kylie Jenner got her some of them
called it a full lip movement,
while the one's that got it honest
were called baboons.
Bodies and faces exaggerated,
distorted for their viewing pleasure
while wide life bearing hips
are used to make us feel ashamed.
Let them tell it, another white girl
changed the game with her shit.
Lips and hips,
breasts and derrieres
are their greatest and newest assets
yet we were told to lose some.
I guess it only benefits when you're the white,
I mean the right, complexion.
It's a complex, son.
The justice system keeps us
unbalanced on their scales,
empty entire clips in our backs
yet don't understand our wails,
can't fathom why we'd want to protest,
why we're sick of being guilty
of driving while black... or brown.
Minorities subjected to stop and frisks
and it don't matter if you don't
ascribe to the stereotypes

or define yourself as "ethnic",
falling short of white simply makes you a target.
This land of the free wasn't made for you.
Though made by you, a history of your blood,
sweat and tears, there's no telling
when you'd reap the benefits of your labor.
The only affirmative action is guns drawn,
137 rounds of ammo unleashed
into your already wrecked car.
If you aren't dead you'd best believe they'll kill you,
shoot you on the ground and handcuff your corpse.
Sever your spine and pretend to try to heal you despite knowing your
mortal soul is beyond repair.
Putting holes in our bodies and spirits,
burying and/or planting evidence,
messing with our minds.
Have us believing we need to straighten our hair,
bleach our complexions because they can't handle the sweetness here in
these blackberries.
Our juice is too sweet so they give us toxins and bitters known as labels,
stereotypes and boxes we have to check off to remove doubts that we're a
threat.
They're always watching,
just waiting on us to revolt for what they did;
what their system is doing.
They'd rather believe we just pat our weaves,
suck our teeth,
collect food stamps,
rob liquor stores and drink forties,
and make babies we can't raise on minimum wage...
at least that's what they'll have you believe.

Transracial

Sometimes I feel Transracial.
No, really.
I get confused about what box I'm supposed to fit in,
If I'm supposed to fit into a box at all.
I ask myself questions like:
How African am I?
How American am I?
Am I really Haitian since I was born in the Bahamas?
Does it matter if the Bahamian government never recognized me as a
Bahamian?
Am I just another naturalized American citizen rich in melanin?
it's unclear just where I fit in because I'm sure it takes
more than speaking creole or eating bannann peze & griot to be Haitian.
Is it enough to eat soup joumou on the first of the year?
Eat my diri kole?
I'm still living while Black so does my Haitian-ness matter anyway?
Experience has taught me that the way I'm perceived in many cases changes
when I open my mouth.
People are different shades of curious or hateful-
few I've found indifferent but maybe that depends on who I'm with.
I get requests like:
"Say something in Kreyol"
or "nah, we don't like Haitians ".
Cool as the black friend until
I get a call from my mama and my Haitian slips in,
I mean Kreyol.
No, not Louisiana.
No, my cuisine is not Cajun.
I'm curious as to why when
it's discovered that I'm Haitian
I am asked if I make jerk chicken?
I mean, my mama might but

I kind of thought that was Jamaican...
Yes, I know that's ignorant.
Am I black enough?
I mean I *really* enjoy pop and country music...
I get made to feel like those genres
are "white people exclusive".
Am I Transracial?
I'm asking, seriously.
I know that I am a culmination
of everything that makes me, me.
But what does that mean?

Chasing Dragons

You.
You are my syringe full of heroin
that I'd gladly catch a case for.
Elastic bands of your fingertips pinch my skin 'til it's bruised but I've
gotta get you in my system.
I'm itching to shoot up, gotta get a dose of your love.
I'd withstand the pain that burns my veins 'cuz I know,
that it leads to a haze that swallows up this emptiness and leaves me with
bliss.
Let me taste your tongue.
Bite my lips,
Leave them swollen and bruised from your kisses.
Bruised tattoos leave me weightless.
Wrap me in your caress; lend me your warmth.
The depths of your eyes are leave me exposed.
Awaken my soul with your sensual touch.
Tap my heart like fingers tap syringe,
full and heavy of hope for this black and white
to embrace different hues.
Color my world.
Whisper your psychedelic fantasies in my ear as I steady the beats of my
kaleidoscope heart.
Let your fingers take hold of me
as my eyelids droop and my breathing slows.
Stroke my secret places,
I grant you safe passage just rescue me.
Whispered moans escape me as you slowly creep in.
Seize hold of my veins
as if poison and antidote collide.
If I could smoke you, I would.
Burn my fingertips
'til I could inhale every spark of you.

Fill me with every inch of you,
push and pull;
move in sync with the fire running through me.
I am content.
I have tasted your medicine and floated on dreams of a high well spent on
my trip to you.
I am lifted by the taste of you.
Butterfly kisses on my skin feel like lighter on spoon
I get hotter, hotter, and pliable.
I can hear your heartbeat
reverberating in my eardrums,
I can feel you deep to my core.
Rock and exhaust me.
Lull me to sleep.
Take me higher.
Color me beautiful and paint me yours.

Heartbreak Kid

He was a crack baby,
He said he had a hard time
with his addiction to drugs.
She was a heartbreak baby.
Her struggle's with love,
the ever-elusive dragon they keep chasing.
He made mention of a different lifetime,
alluded to different outcomes
and she said "yeah but we're here and there's only one that I want to be
with".
He laughed, sure that she has said that before.
She laughed but couldn't tell him he was wrong.
She was definitely chasing that dragon.
Looking for that high.
That ideal love,
not just a lover part time,
but looking for love had a habit of
setting her up for failure.
Years later, she was still learning
salvation takes divine intervention.
She embraced that life is a lesson
and love is like an ocean;
It takes some navigation to explore
those uncharted waters.
Lord help her, she's easily swallowed up by a dazzling smile and a deep
hello.
Like/Lust/love = an almost invisible addiction.
No one really sees the effects
the yearning leaves on the heart
when you've been starved until you tell them.
They can see the tremors in the hands of the alcoholic;
See the yearning in the eyes of the crack fiend or cocaine addict.

Stereotype the kleptomaniac behavior
and probably narrow down
their withdrawal symptoms to the days.
They can see track marks of heroin
or spot a junkie by the haze,
tell by the scars on a cutter
that they're addicted to the pain
but you can't really *see*
the telltale signs of love junkie.
Can you?
Can you count the number
of reckless relationships or fantasies?
Can you determine if it's the party life
or the solidarity?
Drinking as a coping skill or drinking as a means?
Is it multiple partners or
same partner with high frequency?
Is it a search for sex or intimacy?
What does the heartbreak kid look like?

Insecure

I am masked insecurity at its finest.
I hate the way I look so I place dark shadows over my eyelids,
hoping the darkness deflects my pain.
I'm trying to disguise my misery with things
like laughing in the rain
and sadly,
my bluff is working.
'cause you're not looking.
At least you're not looking close enough to see me.
I laugh out loud releasing silent screams
and maybe if you paid attention to the signs,
just maybe,
you'd notice me here dying.
Perhaps the truth is you do see
but you're just fighting your battles too.
Fighting to hide the same insecurities.

Rider

I've got your back
No slipped discs,
26+ vertebrae
I'm continually present to show my support.
I know it's difficult to share your thoughts
as the bills and stress add up,
But no matter how the weight of the world
threatens to crush your lumbar,
I know your tailbone's strong;
Cervical spine on point,
Together we'll find the balance.
And on the days when the pressure threatens to crush your hopes,
I want you to know,
I'll share mine with you.
I've got your thoracic.
So, go ahead and keep that chest poked out,
sacrum sacred,
and that smirk on your face.
We'll take all the L's we need to secure the win.
I'll be your back brace;
I've got your back, babe.

Collide With Me

Let us run a crash course
that sends us exploding into each other.
Lose ourselves in the rich texture of each other's skin,
blending skin tones, intertwining fingertips.
Orbiting outside of our respective galaxies only to connect and re-create
life forms.
Stars bursting as we touch, skies crying, releasing massive orgasmic
storms.
Whispers that resonate like thunder.
Our movements as swift and captivating like cracks of lightning as we
kiss forms.
Connecting and disengaging.
Constructing and destroying.
Removing our souls from the devils grasp and hiding them in each
other, as we touch nerves.
Plant yourself in the depths of my genetic code and never again need to
seek refuge.
I'm here to rescue you from falling out of orbit.
Lose yourself in me
so I can remind you where to find it,
and even though we're crashing,
I hope that we collide.
If even for a millisecond, I hope we lock eyes,
getting off course to become each other's target.
Let's connect lives before we hit the stratosphere,
let's share life, and live it.
Never mind coasting,
let's push ourselves to the limit and collide.
Collide with me.

Dashes, Hyphens, & Minuses

Dashes
A horizontal stroke in writing or printing to mark a pause. Hyphens
The sign -, used to join words to indicate that they have a combined
meaning, break in sense.
Minus sign
A mathematical symbol meaning to subtract.
The same sign on a tombstone or grave marker gives pause,
tells a story.
Sentences left unfinished,
Lives cut short,
Lives lived long.
Tales of love,
of self,
of family,
alone or accompanied or lost.
Successes and failures,
one dash can tell a tale from beginning to end.
It recounts memories.
Tragedies.
History.
Heart wrenching accounts of love.
Hard work and gain.
Losses and pains.
Kisses and hugs.
Maybe even the absence of
but they say something.
Everything about how you lived,
who you've left,
Who's waiting.
The things you've done,
lives you've touched,
or didn't.

Sometimes they say nothing
those dashes.
They can be loud though silent;
A pregnant pause
leaving room for more
until your date of death follows.
Time is not promised
and that line is simply a reminder.
What will yours say?

Rhythm

The beat drops and I'm carried away
floating on lyrics whose meanings change every time I hear them.
They get deeper or clearer,
and when I turn down the bass enough it's usually both.
Music videos my imagination has directed play on in my mind.
The people dance freely.
They feel it.
The need to break free,
no apologies for feeling, they just dance.
Like David did and I smile.
Every burden unhinged from their spines,
they shake, gouye, twerk,
pop, lock, krump,
kompa, pirouette,
there are no limits to the way their feet move.
No, in this church, they are no statues,
everybody gets lifted.
For me this is liberty.
I can feel it in the reverb.
I listen intently to the lyrics
and hit repeat so I can catch them again.
Just in case I've missed something.
Every song has a meaning.
You just have to let yourself feel it
What rhythm are you living to?

Calls

My heart breaks every time I get a call
and it's someone who's loved so hard
but was abandoned.
Someone who put all of their love eggs
into one basket
only to discover that there was a hole somewhere.
When I hear the unshed tears
struggling to be kept at bay slowly break
through the surface,
I charge my heart to be strong enough
for the both of us;
call it counter transference
but there's something about the heartbreak of souls...
Something about holding on so tightly,
for so long and being forced to let go
that leaves fingers and hearts achy;
palms and souls tired.
Waking up to discover that love is not enough
and/or shouldering all of the blame on your own.
The beep comes in
and sometimes I get mad at the phone
because I can hear brokenness
in the first 5 seconds of silence.
I hope that somehow
I can find some words that'll convey it'll be okay
when it feels like it won't;
when living feels like drowning,
loving feels like suffocation
and asking for help tastes like acid
on the tip of the tongue.
Heavy hearts in call waiting.
Tears stuck in the queue.

Despair spilling out over keyboards
and you know that there's a bridge between
you and the bruises on the line
and while you know the importance of lending an ear
the only solace you can offer is "I'm here",
though not really
because you're boxed in by protocols.
Call lights blink signaling
there are other calls to get to;
other requests in the queue
but these are ones that tear at me.
They haunt me,
these calls.

Grieve

I didn't grieve you.
I don't think I knew how to
or what to do with a love that profound.
A love so unraveling; redefining.
A love that created and consumed a phoenix all in the same breath-
that stretched my teenage heart.
I don't think we were ready.
How could we be?
Barely old enough to go to war,
or to know what was worth fighting for,
afraid of our shadows.
Of our demons,
of our capacity to love and be loved.
How were we to know how to process "us"
when we barely had a grasp on "me"?
I know I didn't.
Or did I?
Did I know me enough to know you would haunt me?
That I would have wanted to bring your seed to life?
Would that have been a reality?
What if….
What if's….
I thought I had you buried.
Dealt with the loss as we grew separately,
processed the treachery of teenage emotions.
They were bigger than me, those feelings.
So gigantic but I still tried to carry them on my own.
Did you feel it, too?
Were you scared?
Tell me, was it real?
I want to believe that it was

because surely a figment of my imagination wouldn't cling to me this
much,
wouldn't come back as faded memories with feelings this clear.
I remember you in stillness.
As clear as crystal,
my heart remembers the echoes of us
when I hear your voice,
These mini panic attacks leave me shook.
Scared.
I fought so hard not remember
and contact after all these years
has me remembering things that I shouldn't.
I thought I had you buried
but remnants of you linger still...
Your breathing jogs memories.
My mind has blocks
but this antenna of your feelings
is causing static where there used to be white noise.
This, this present is peaceful.
The future I have planned is within reach,
so why is my curiosity of what could have been gnawing at me?
I know what we were!
A lesson
A practice round
A messy,
blissful,
complex,
fragile thing.
A first love that gave me everything
and nothing at all.
Although my limbs remember our fall,
I also remember all the time I've spent untangling,
getting upright again.
I don't want to feel that frazzled or lost
ever
again.

Love Him Like...

Imagine a joy so overwhelming.
Like the one the Gulf's Fishermen would find if we could rewind time,
and BP never had that oil spill.
Envision a world so evolved,
That we actually ceased slavery, segregation and racism;
A time in which we destroyed all the bloodshed between gangs and innocents
and somehow won the war on drugs.
I love him that much.
Can you dig it?
Deep trenches in the Middle East that hate could never know.
Legalization of marijuana so those cataracts and tumors would recede in growth;
A cure for cancer that grants the future a chance to meet people it may have otherwise never known,
or maybe even a solution to this genocide.
The discovery of the HIV/Aids cure.
I love him like a long-awaited breakthrough.
Like a battle plan that doesn't involve the death of our soldiers or the loss of children that would never be.
A solution that ends with peace all across the globe,
a love as strong as the spirit of New Orleans,
a faith so strong that even an earthquake or tsunami couldn't breach, or destroy it.
Love him like I'd love to see an end to the need of Feed the Children commercials,
I'm telling you I love him this much.
I love him like I wish Desert Storm never happened.
Like how Jesus fed the multitude off a meager basket.
Like a Cruciverbalist loves to make crosswords.
My love for him is endless.
Epic like the Iliad and the Odyssey.

Love him more than boy bands
love to rock their skinny jeans,
Yeah, I love him like that.
Like I cherish the silence between every heartbeat and the steady thud
that follows,
Knowing our time here is never guaranteed 'cause our time is only
borrowed.
I love him like I love to breathe.
I love him.
Even in the midst of uncertainty.

Joy

I laughed so hard today
Didn't think I could laugh that hard
but his smile and mirth are contagious
Belly laughter had me shed mad calories,
His laugh is protein and vitamins for my hungry soul
I can't even remember what he said
but I remember being pulled into his side,
feeling my rib slide into the empty space in his ribcage;
the spot I was birthed from
Feeling his hands rest on my side
Protective
Protected
Possessive
Like this is mine
Territory marked forever
And we whispered
tangled in the covers
about breakfast
and last night
and this morning
I told him he's beautiful mid yawn
He said I was snoring
I told him it's his fault for making me happy
He said there's no correlation because I snore when I'm mad too
Told me to stop making up stories
Indignantly I told him I'm a lady
and ladies don't snore
even if we curse like sailors
We laughed some more
I stole a kiss
I live for those kinds of moments

Ode to Andre

In the words of Jade Andwele,
"I will write you poem, after poem, after poem".
I will write you love letters
Professing my love for you
My respect for you
My awe of and pride in you
At least one a month for the rest of our lives
I will tell you of all of the ways you are adored
I will pen, pencil, sharpie-- draw out all of the feels
I will keep chronicle of how "us" feels
Even when I may not be feeling it
I commit.
To you
To me
To us
This love
I will love you even when it hurts
I will leave you love notes in the form of kisses on cheeks
On forehead
On eyelid
On lips
On chest
In caress
In listening to the rhythm of your heartbeat
I will sway to the bass of your drums
And hum
And dance
And laugh
I will sing
All of Solomon's songs
My beloved, I will love you
I will sing you

I will feel you
And nurture your heart
Nourish your soul
Listening with intent
Hesitant to speak
Unless I'm speaking life
into and unto you
I will love you beyond where the sidewalk ends
I will love you in the glow of the sun
And in the cold of the moon
I will love you in action
In braille
In rhythm
In color
In taste
In sound
In touch
In sight
In love
I will love you for the rest of my life
I will love you in scripture
And in stars
With these arms,
These hands,
These legs,
These feet,
This heart
With every fiber of my being
I will love you in thought
I will love you in words
I will love you like verb
And I will write you poem
After poem
After poem

Words...

There are these words
Words that I wish could travel on whispers to him and hug his heart.
Words like bandages and sutures.
Erasers and glue.
Words that haven't been put into the right sequences yet.
Me…
You…
There are these words.
Words that remain unspoken,
as feelings get unchecked
because to confess the depth of what they mean
could require priests and rosary beads coupled with "Hail Mary's".
Words that impose the 5th Amendment
because I pled the fifth when I asked myself where this was going;
where the words
you, *me*, **us**,
could lead to…
I wanted to hold the words.
Hold them like my memories hold his kisses…
like the secrets theses walls hold,
they are not at liberty to reveal our secrets
Words like *rules* and *lust*…
Love and trust,
words that cause a blush of deep hues on coy cheeks, a flush of warm heat,
words like *taboo* and *forgive* me,
I find it hard to resist the pull of his words.
Pronouns and verbs…
He makes me want to take action;
show him better than I can tell him
how *jealous* I am of his teeth and his lips.
I'm jealous of his spit.
What I'd give to be close to his <u>tongue</u>…

To *feel* the delivery of his words.
I'd like to tip toe around in his brain
so I can be present for the birth of his words
and lie in the bubbles of his thoughts…
Shadow his memory,
discover the words he reserves for me,
if only I could see the color scheme of his alphabet.
What I'd give to be the throat that envelope's his words and the chords
to his vocal…
the **bass** that escapes his esophagus,
the *calligraphy* he produces without pens…
There are these words.
Words I keep <u>hidden</u> because
I *fear* they will be ignored,
unnoticed, or misunderstood.
Words that convey more than I'm willing to *confess*.
Words that have yet to be spoken
but move me nonetheless.
There's power in these silent,
unmatched, unspoken words.
They keep tongue in cheek,
hiding behind protective walls of ivory,
whimpering as they are about to be pushed out
and past lips and free fall into the atmosphere.
As they are spoken,
they quietly whisper their fear of being broken and empty.
They beg to land on the cushion of understanding
and acceptance as they land at his feet.
They are mere words.
Holding the promise of everything…
There are these **words**.

If Walls Could Talk

I'm not good at math
but I've learned to count somethings
like the number of beings in my space.
The number of laughs and arguments,
slammed doors and times the doors are left open,
I think I'm good at counting the creaks of the stairs.
There are always at least four feet running up and down them.
I'm good at listening to spoken and unspoken words,
there are a lot of them here.
I do not know science.
Short of the bodily functions I've witnessed
I couldn't tell you how organic beings work.
I do not know geography.
I could not tell you exactly where I am in the grand scheme of things,
but I can tell you the number and letter on the door.
And it's color. It is green.
There are rooms where my people sleep,
a space where they sometimes unsuccessfully create
meals, and there are items on the floor.
I believe that they are called toys?
There is also something that growls often,
smells strange and waters the yard,
but my people seem to enjoy its company.
The number of people varies but they are the same.
There are big ones and small ones and
the smaller ones seem to make the most noise.
I do not mind them.
They keep me company.
I've heard them refer to themselves as "family".
They usually refer to me as "inside", "house" and "home".
I like it when they call me the latter, the most.

Energy (A Poem for Morales)

We are all energy-
Powerhouses of love and promise,
Culminations of memories and moments-
That keep us immortal
Even when we shed our skin and return it to dust,
Our souls remain capable of touch;
Capable of shaping the beings around us
We still laugh
and cry
and dance
and sing in the memories of those who loved
and knew us best.
Even in the minds and hearts of
once in a lifetime acquaintances
memories are kept alive
and in memories we thrive-
There's no escaping or erasing energy;
it's simply redistributed
Embrace it
Close your eyes
Breathe in and feel the breath in your lungs
Catch his whispers on your exhale,
Feel his smile in the corners of your eyes
as they crinkle,
Hear him in the timbre or jingle of your laughter-
Weep not,
because in his final chapter he found peace
Feel him in the stillness;
In the playful voices of children
In the rebellion of teenage angst
In the complexities that color adulthood
and know that he is still with you,

swaying painlessly in the wind, listening...
Let his warmth kiss the top of your head
like rays from the sun
Hear him in the lilt of your voice
as you disperse pearls of wisdom
and when you feel sad,
when his loss feels too heavy to bear,
Know that there are so many arms
willing to hold you-
Ears willing to listen to your stories of him,
Hearts willing to grieve and grow because of his love-
Willing to catch and hold your tears as they fall.
As you release your grief,
exhale
He's at peace, love.
Find your smile,
Hold on to it
and let his love shine through.

Call Center Resources

A stranger called, wanting me to have all the answers.
Wanted me to tell him which branch of service he should join and I
informed him that I couldn't.
He said he just wanted to make a difference,
didn't care about the perks or benefits,
he just wanted to be a man of uniform…
Went to school, got a degree in business
but wasn't certain where he should go.
No military family to help him choose
so he just wanted to know more.
I directed him to some resources and advised him to get in touch with a
recruiter.
He said he had but they all came off like they worked in sales and tried to
sell him their branch.
He said he wanted someone impartial,
I told him I was a bit biased, being prior Navy.
We laughed & I told him to trust his gut
He said he wasn't sure
although he was leading towards the Corps,
& I told him it sounded like he decided.
Still he said he wasn't sure,
so was looking to me for guidance.
I had no answers.
Save for knowing that
you don't have to enlist to make a difference.
He asked about my service,
specifically asked why I chose it.
Told him I wanted out of my city &
out of my mama's house—
I just wanted to be free.
(I left out that I picked that branch because of a crush
but I told him about my recruiter.)

58

He thanked me for my service
It took a while for me to learn not cringe at the support
usually feeling guilty that I didn't have the best reasons when I joined.
I told him that he should continue to research
the different jobs & opportunities available.
He said he didn't care one way or another
What he did, but he was called to serve.
I told him to listen to his instincts & to go for it.
Then I spent 2 minutes smiling & shaking my head.
I joined for freedom & opportunity,
which any of the branches would have given me
but that one impulse led me to so much growth,
for better and worse it shaped me.

Thank you

This is for the fallen.
This is for the serving.
This is for those living with the scars of their service,
the Vietnam veterans,
who've never gotten a "thank you" for their sacrifice.
The wounded warriors.
Hospitalized heroes.
Post traumatically stressed out vets;
those who can't talk about their mental health
because we've taught them to be stoic and
filled their heads with the lie that soldier's don't cry.
Those we've tried to convince being a soldier means
being too strong to shed tears or admit they're scared.
This is for every soldier who feels broken;
every sailor,
airman,
marine,
guardsman
who wonders if he/she will ever be the same.
This is for the Korean War soldiers
whom we may never know by name...
Service members born in the United States
but treated like aliens all the same...
This is for those proud men
serving their country in WWII,
People of Color segregated because of their skin,
this is for you!
Post 9/11 champion.
Gulf war veteran.
WWI, Cold war and peace time brethren,
those that signed their names on the dotted line,
prepared to make the ultimate sacrifice.

Everyone who's ever donned a uniform and promised to defend this
country from enemies both foreign and domestic,
this is for those who've been exposed to Agent Orange.
For all the amputees.
Those with TBI's, MST, PTSD
all in the name of serving their country.
This is for the homeless vets.
The forgotten.
The ones who drink, smoke, sniff, sex themselves to death trying to cope
with their memories,
fighting off their demons,
trying to forget.
Those who gave it all to Uncle Sam
and have little of themselves left...
The overworked.
The underpaid.
Misunderstood.
Abandoned.
This is for the Machinists sweating in the pit.
The Seabees trudging through ruins.
The Corpsmen tending to the wounded.
The Gunnies providing cover.
The Infantryman in the thick of it.
The Religious Program Specialists
and their Chaplin's
This is for the courageous.
This is for the meek.
Whether pushing papers
or traversing enemy territory,
for every prisoner of war,
and yes, even some deserters too.
This is long overdue.
If you've never been told before,
Let me be the first to say it:
Thank you!

Unfair Trades

They gave me a flag.
Buried you with a 21 gun salute
and every bullet broke my heart.
Every shot fired pulled apart my soul
'cause I could only relive losing you.
Every second taken away from us,
time we would never spend;
Every moment we could have shared,
words that remained unsaid...
They put you in a casket and covered it with a flag.
Bright stars and broad stripes.
Stars that we can no longer gaze at together.
The North Star will never guide you home again.
Stripes of red and white haunt me.
They handed me old glory
and though I love our country, I'd trade it for you.
While they argued over the prices of oil,
they didn't know what you were fighting for,
you fought for freedom.
Blood, sweat, and life force to defend our home
under their false pretense of finding terror's address,
you took rounds of enemy fire deep in your chest
and they put you in a grave and gave me a flag!
The flag that they'd laid on your casket.
Folded up in a triangle and placed in my hand;
a flag for your service.
A token of their appreciation
and a reminder of what you were fighting for,
except they had no clue.
No clue that you just wanted to do your part
in the lingering ashes of September 11th.
No idea that you signed over your life as my forever,

became a guardian and protector,
to ensure a safe future for a nation you believed in.
Politicians that held no regard for your dreams,
just their petroleum fueled agenda
and political schemes,
those gemini like vipers don't even hide in the grass.
They shed their skin behind political parties
and the flags they give.
A flag that destroyed our forever and stole your love.
Faded your whispers.
Left remnants of your hugs
in the form of black and white faint memories
and my mouth longing for your kiss.
They left us this.
This land of the free, home of the brave
with others like me broken,
the other half of our souls trapped in a grave...
They gave us a flag.
Tight stripes and dimming stars.
21 gun salutes and these scars;
this ache that resonates deep in our souls
and a tainted Old Glory at half-mast.
A future that will never happen— all for a flag.
A flag I now hold at night instead of you.
I feel the echo of those rounds,
my stars cry red, white and bruised.
They gave me a flag in exchange for freedom
but I never wanted to be free of you.
I'd give it back if I could.
But they gave me this flag.

Printed in the United States
By Bookmasters